FOOTBALL'S GREATEST STARS

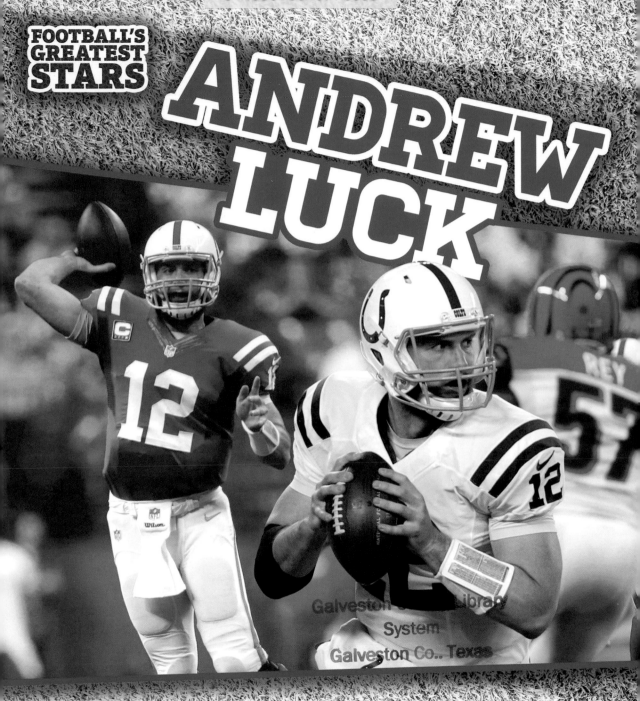

ANDREW LUCK

by Matt Scheff

SportsZone

An Imprint of Abdo Publishing
abdopublishing.com

abdopublishing.com

Published by Abdo Publishing, a division of ABDO, PO Box 398166, Minneapolis, Minnesota 55439. Copyright © 2016 by Abdo Consulting Group, Inc. International copyrights reserved in all countries. No part of this book may be reproduced in any form without written permission from the publisher. SportsZone™ is a trademark and logo of Abdo Publishing.

Printed in the United States of America, North Mankato, Minnesota
052015
092015

Cover Photos: Chris Szagola/AP Images (foreground); AJ Mast/AP Images (background)
Interior Photos: Chris Szagola/AP Images, 1 (foreground); AJ Mast/AP Images, 1 (background), 26-27; Michael Conroy/AP Images, 4-5, 6-7, 22-23; Aaron M. Sprecher/AP Images, 8-9; Margaret Bowles/AP Images, 10-11; Paul Sakuma/AP Images, 12-13, 14, 15, 16-17; Damon Tarver/Cal Sport Media/AP Images, 18-19; Tomasso DeRosa/AP Images, 20; Rick Osentoski/AP Images, 21; Patric Schneider/AP Images, 24-25; Jack Dempsey/AP Images, 28-29

Editor: Nick Rebman
Series Designer: Jake Nordby

Library of Congress Control Number: 2015932399

Cataloging-in-Publication Data
Scheff, Matt.
 Andrew Luck / Matt Scheff.
  p. cm. -- (Football's greatest stars)
Includes index.
ISBN 978-1-62403-825-9
1. Luck, Andrew, 1989- --Juvenile literature. 2. Football players--United States--Biography--Juvenile literature. 3. Quarterbacks (Football)--United States--Biography--Juvenile literature.   I. Title.
796.332092--dc23
[B]   2015932399

CONTENTS

EPIC COMEBACK 4

EARLY LIFE 8

BIG MAN ON CAMPUS 14

REPLACING A LEGEND 20

COMING UP CLUTCH 24

Timeline 30
Glossary 31
Index 32

EPIC COMEBACK

Quarterback Andrew Luck's first home playoff game could not have started much worse. The game was in January 2014, and Luck's Indianapolis Colts trailed the Kansas City Chiefs 38-10 in the third quarter. It seemed like a disaster.

Then everything changed. Luck zipped passes all over the field. He hit running back Donald Brown with a touchdown pass. Then he found tight end Coby Fleener for another score. Luck even ran in a fumble.

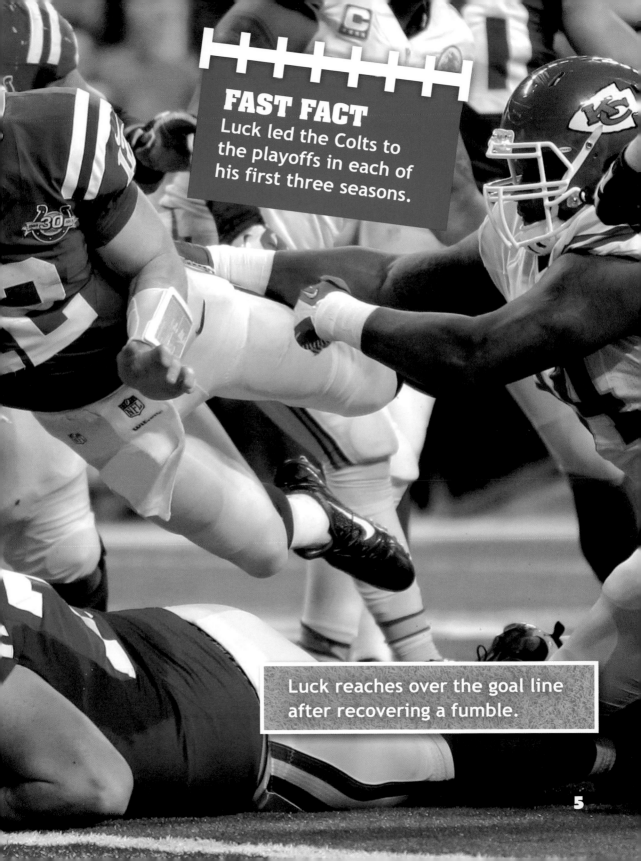

Luck reaches over the goal line after recovering a fumble.

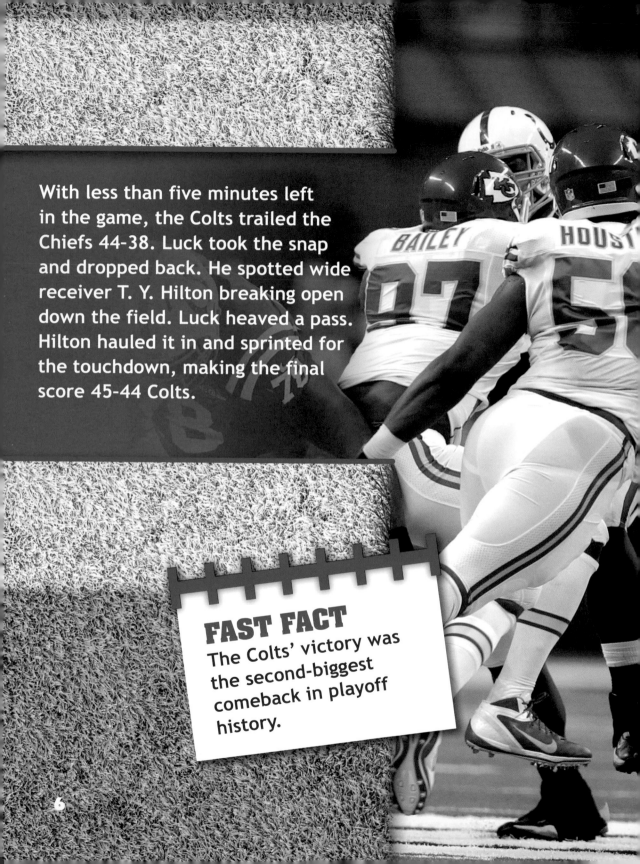

With less than five minutes left in the game, the Colts trailed the Chiefs 44-38. Luck took the snap and dropped back. He spotted wide receiver T. Y. Hilton breaking open down the field. Luck heaved a pass. Hilton hauled it in and sprinted for the touchdown, making the final score 45-44 Colts.

FAST FACT

The Colts' victory was the second-biggest comeback in playoff history.

Luck throws a pass downfield as he leads the Colts to a playoff victory against the Chiefs.

EARLY LIFE

Andrew Luck was born on September 12, 1989, in Washington, DC. Football was in his blood. His dad, Oliver, had been a star quarterback in college and played in the National Football League (NFL).

During the 1990s, Andrew's father got a job in Europe. So Andrew grew up in London, England, and Frankfurt, Germany.

Andrew plays in a 2006 game with Stratford High School.

9

FAST FACT

Andrew's father, Oliver, helped run the World League of American Football.

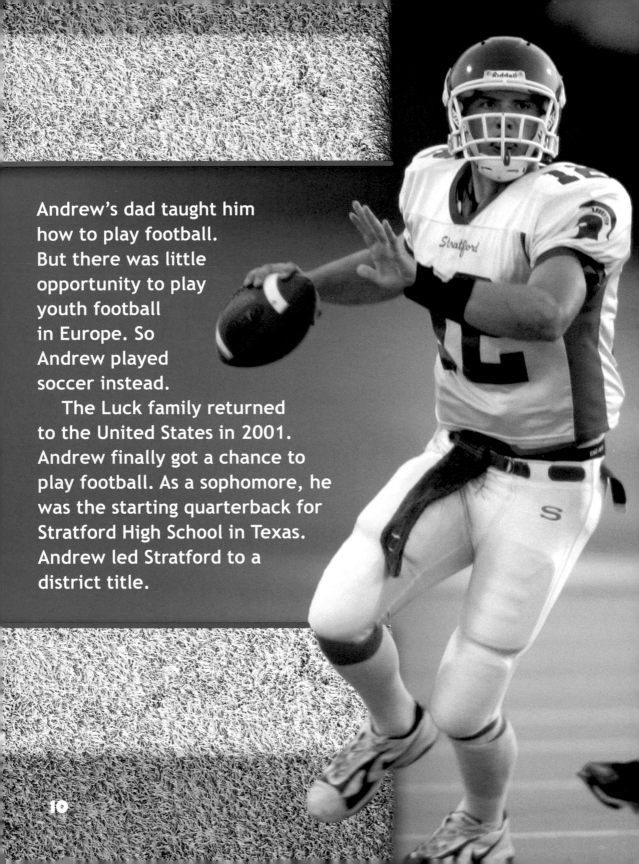

Andrew's dad taught him how to play football. But there was little opportunity to play youth football in Europe. So Andrew played soccer instead.

The Luck family returned to the United States in 2001. Andrew finally got a chance to play football. As a sophomore, he was the starting quarterback for Stratford High School in Texas. Andrew led Stratford to a district title.

Andrew escapes from a defender during a high school football game in Texas.

FAST FACT

Soccer is the most popular sport in Europe. Luck remains a big soccer fan today.

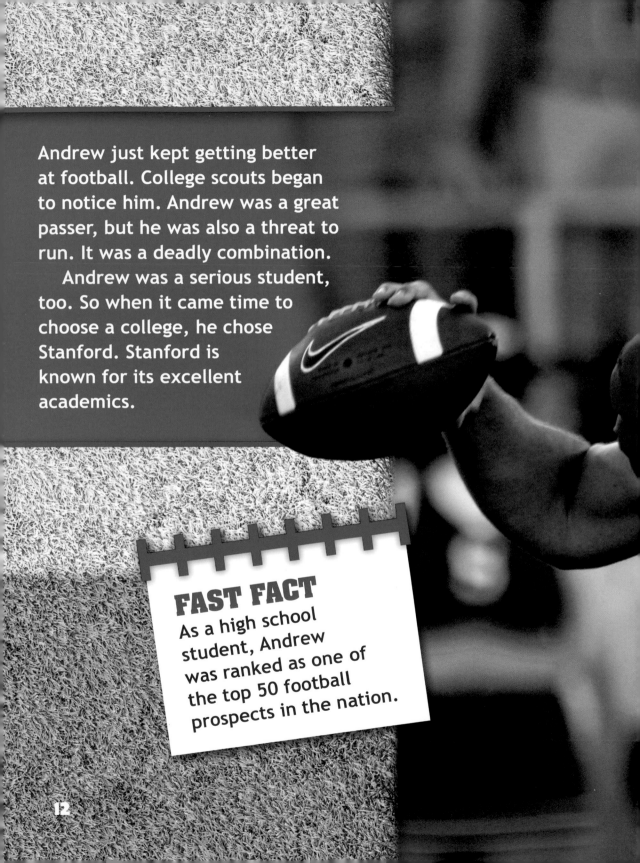

Andrew just kept getting better at football. College scouts began to notice him. Andrew was a great passer, but he was also a threat to run. It was a deadly combination.

Andrew was a serious student, too. So when it came time to choose a college, he chose Stanford. Stanford is known for its excellent academics.

FAST FACT

As a high school student, Andrew was ranked as one of the top 50 football prospects in the nation.

Luck passes the ball in a 2009 game at Stanford Stadium.

BIG MAN ON CAMPUS

Stanford seemed like an odd choice to some. The school's football team had won only five games in the previous two seasons. But Luck believed in the university's new coach, Jim Harbaugh.

Luck redshirted in his first year at Stanford. He concentrated on his studies. Then in 2009, he took over as the team's starting quarterback.

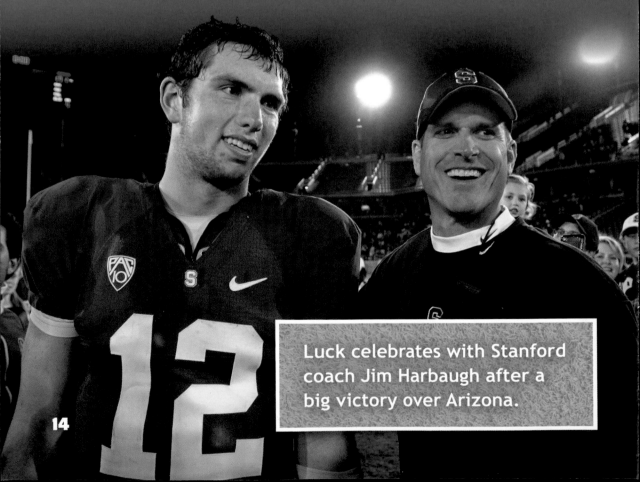

Luck celebrates with Stanford coach Jim Harbaugh after a big victory over Arizona.

FAST FACT
Luck studied architectural design in college.

Luck eludes a pass rush in a 2010 game.

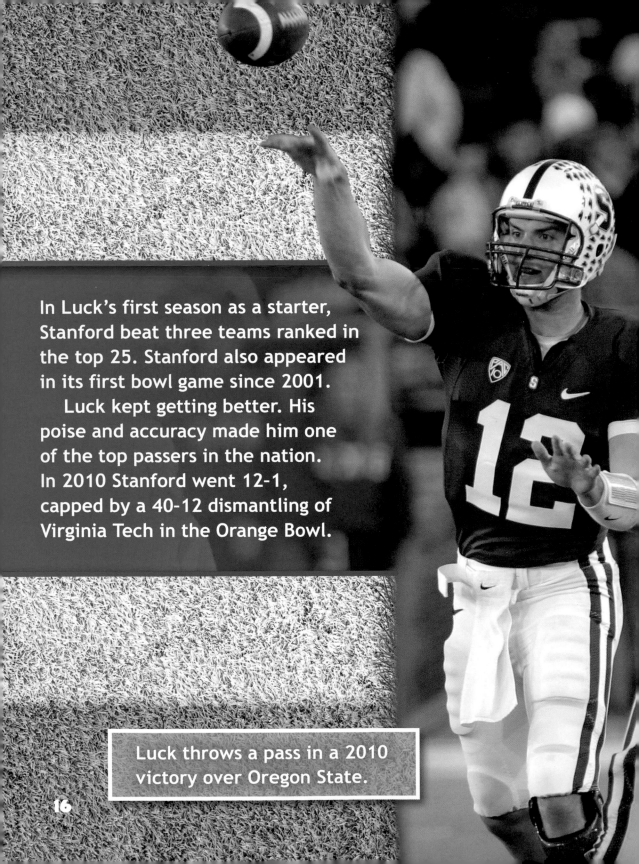

In Luck's first season as a starter, Stanford beat three teams ranked in the top 25. Stanford also appeared in its first bowl game since 2001.

Luck kept getting better. His poise and accuracy made him one of the top passers in the nation. In 2010 Stanford went 12-1, capped by a 40-12 dismantling of Virginia Tech in the Orange Bowl.

Luck throws a pass in a 2010 victory over Oregon State.

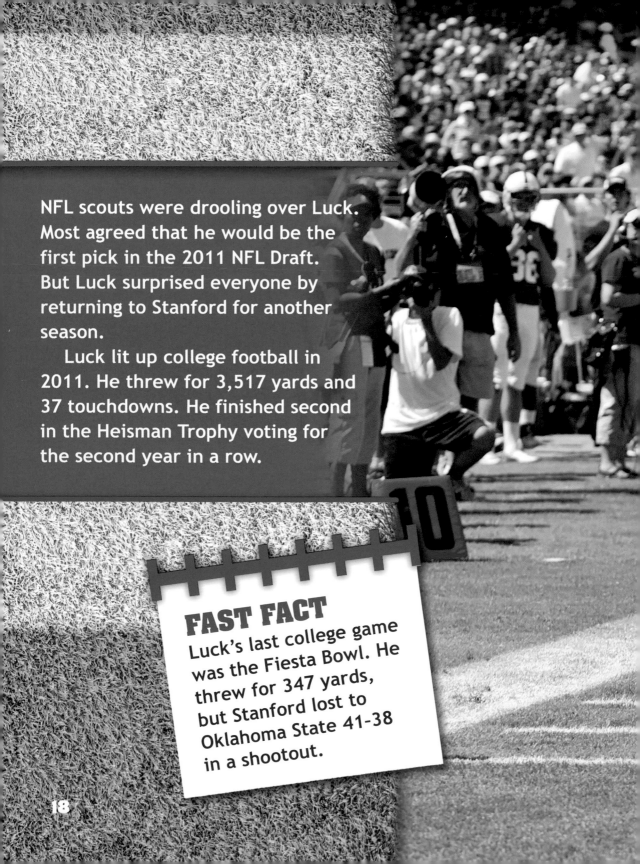

NFL scouts were drooling over Luck. Most agreed that he would be the first pick in the 2011 NFL Draft. But Luck surprised everyone by returning to Stanford for another season.

Luck lit up college football in 2011. He threw for 3,517 yards and 37 touchdowns. He finished second in the Heisman Trophy voting for the second year in a row.

FAST FACT
Luck's last college game was the Fiesta Bowl. He threw for 347 yards, but Stanford lost to Oklahoma State 41-38 in a shootout.

Luck reaches for the goal line in a game against San Jose State in 2011.

REPLACING A LEGEND

Luck was ready for the next level. He entered the 2012 NFL Draft. The Colts took him with the first overall pick.

Luck had long been a fan of Colts quarterback Peyton Manning. The Colts had let Manning go after the 2011 season. Luck's job was to replace an NFL legend.

Luck, *right*, poses with NFL Commissioner Roger Goodell after being selected as the first overall pick in the 2012 NFL Draft.

Luck passes the ball against the Detroit Lions during his rookie season.

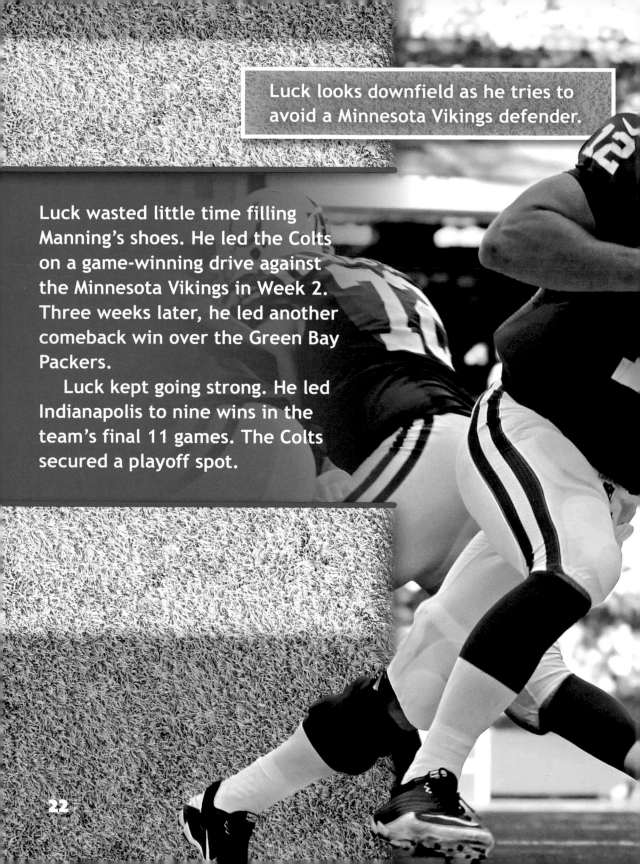

Luck looks downfield as he tries to avoid a Minnesota Vikings defender.

Luck wasted little time filling Manning's shoes. He led the Colts on a game-winning drive against the Minnesota Vikings in Week 2. Three weeks later, he led another comeback win over the Green Bay Packers.

Luck kept going strong. He led Indianapolis to nine wins in the team's final 11 games. The Colts secured a playoff spot.

FAST FACT
Luck's 4,374 passing yards in 2012 were the most ever by a rookie.

COMING UP CLUTCH

In 2013 Luck cemented his status as a clutch quarterback. He always seemed to be at his best in the biggest moments. Luck led four Colts comebacks during the regular season. But he saved the best comeback for the playoffs. The Colts overcame a 28-point deficit to beat the Chiefs.

FAST FACT

Luck threw for 443 yards in the playoff game against Kansas City. That was the fifth-highest playoff total in NFL history.

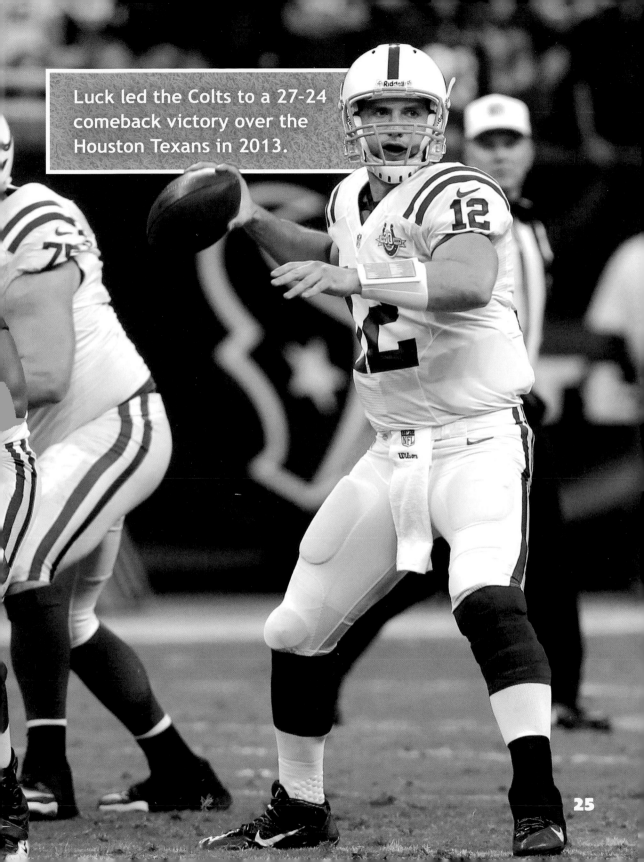

Luck led the Colts to a 27-24 comeback victory over the Houston Texans in 2013.

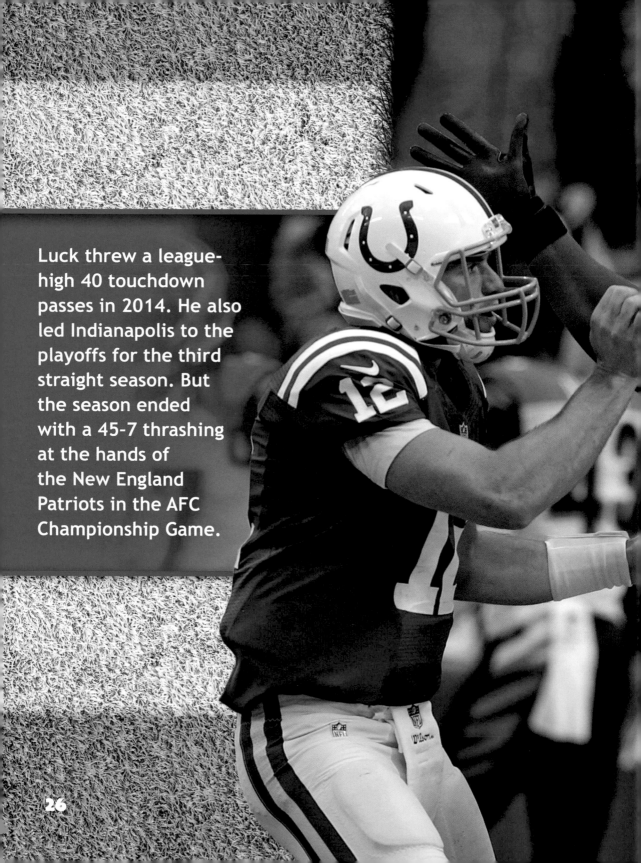

Luck threw a league-high 40 touchdown passes in 2014. He also led Indianapolis to the playoffs for the third straight season. But the season ended with a 45-7 thrashing at the hands of the New England Patriots in the AFC Championship Game.

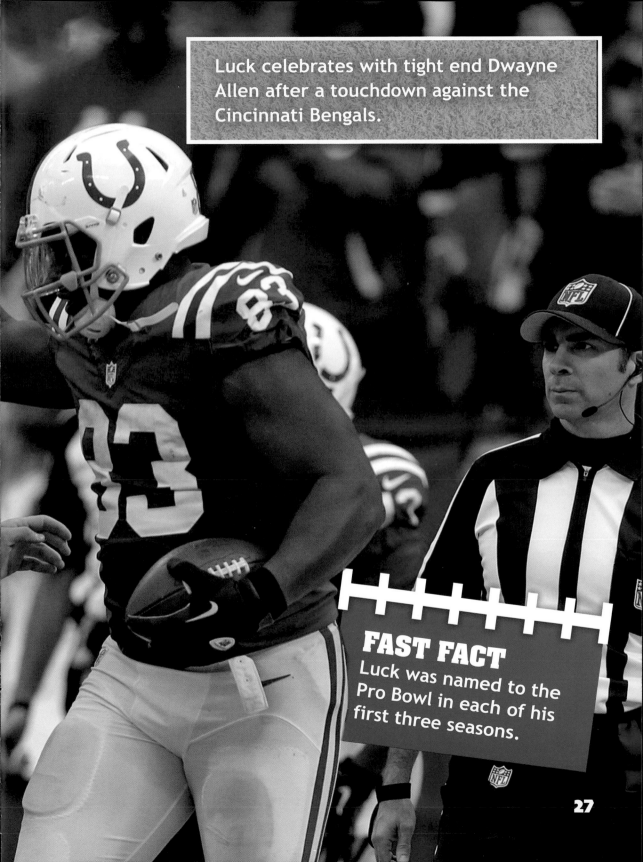

Luck celebrates with tight end Dwayne Allen after a touchdown against the Cincinnati Bengals.

FAST FACT
Luck was named to the Pro Bowl in each of his first three seasons.

Most quarterbacks struggle early in their careers. It takes them time to learn the NFL game and adjust to its speed. But Luck has been a star from the moment he stepped onto an NFL field.

What does the future hold? With Luck's intelligence and athletic ability, there is no telling what he might accomplish.

Luck calls a play in a January 2015 playoff game against the Denver Broncos.

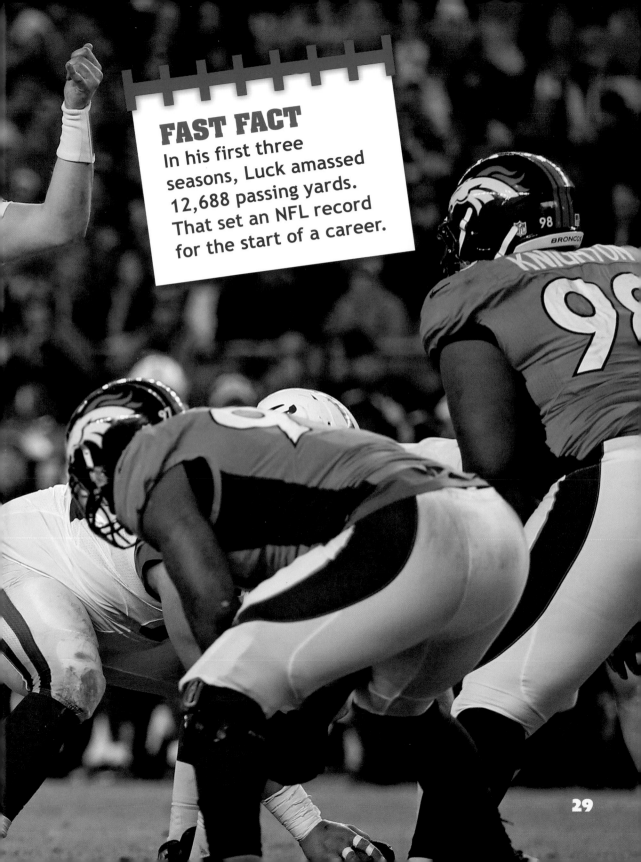

FAST FACT

In his first three seasons, Luck amassed 12,688 passing yards. That set an NFL record for the start of a career.

TIMELINE

1989
Andrew Luck is born on September 12 in Washington, DC.

2001
Luck's family moves from Europe to Texas.

2009
Luck takes over as Stanford's starting quarterback.

2010
Stanford goes 11-1 in the regular season and then wins the Orange Bowl.

2011
Luck finishes second in the Heisman Trophy voting for the second straight season.

2012
The Indianapolis Colts select Luck first overall in the NFL Draft. He goes on to set a rookie passing yardage record and leads the Colts to the playoffs.

2013
The Colts go 11-5 in the regular season and win the AFC South title.

2014
Luck leads the NFL in touchdown passes with 40 and leads the Colts to the AFC Championship Game.

GLOSSARY

ACADEMICS
The pursuit of education.

ARCHITECTURAL DESIGN
The study of buildings and how they are planned.

HEISMAN TROPHY
An honor given to the top college football player each season.

POISE
The ability to remain calm under pressure.

PROSPECT
An athlete likely to succeed at the next level.

REDSHIRT
To practice with a college team but not be allowed to play in any games for one season.

ROOKIE
A first-year player.

SCOUT
A person whose job is to look for talented young players.

INDEX

AFC Championship
  Game, 26

Brown, Donald, 4

Europe, 8, 10, 11

Fiesta Bowl, 18
Fleener, Coby, 4
Frankfurt, Germany, 8

Green Bay Packers, 22

Harbaugh, Jim, 14
Heisman Trophy, 18
Hilton, T. Y., 6

Indianapolis Colts, 4,
  5, 6, 20, 21, 22, 24,
  26

Kansas City Chiefs, 4,
  6, 24

London, England, 8
Luck, Oliver, 8, 9

Manning, Peyton, 20,
  21, 22
Minnesota Vikings, 22

New England Patriots,
  26
NFL Draft, 18, 20

Oklahoma State, 18
Orange Bowl, 16, 17

Pro Bowl, 27

Stanford, 12, 14, 16,
  18
Stratford High School,
  10

Texas, 10

Virginia Tech, 16

Washington, DC, 8
World League of
  American Football, 9

ABOUT THE AUTHOR

Matt Scheff is an artist and author living in Alaska. He enjoys mountain climbing, deep-sea fishing, and curling up with his two Siberian huskies to watch football.